CHAPTER 97 ··· ONCE AGAIN, HACHIMAN HIKIGAYA MAKES A SPEECH. (PART ONE)

CHAPTER 97 ··· ONCE AGAIN, HACHIMAN HIKIGAYA MAKES A SPEECH. (PART ONE)

Cover illustration for
Monthly Sunday GX,
June 2021 issue

MY YOUTH ROMANTIC COMEDY IS WRONG, AS I EXPECTED @comic

18

Original Story
Wataru Watari

Art
Naomichi Io

Character Design
Ponkan⑧

MY YOUTH ROMANTIC COMEDY IS WRONG, AS I EXPECTED @COMIC

CHARACTERS + STORY SO FAR

HACHIMAN HIKIGAYA

LONER AND A TWISTED HUMAN BEING. FORCED TO JOIN THE SERVICE CLUB. ASPIRES TO BE A HOUSEHUSBAND.

YUKINO YUKINOSHITA

PERFECT SUPERWOMAN WITH TOP GRADES AND FLAWLESS LOOKS, BUT HER PERSONALITY AND BOOBS ARE A LETDOWN. PRESIDENT OF THE SERVICE CLUB.

YUI YUIGAHAMA

LIGHT-BROWN HAIR, MINISKIRT, LARGE-BOOBED SLUTTY TYPE. BUT SHE'S ACTUALLY A VIRGIN!? MEMBER OF THE SERVICE CLUB.

IROHA ISSHIKI

SOCCER CLUB ASSISTANT. FIRST-YEAR.

SAIKA TOTSUKA

THE SINGLE FLOWER BLOOMING IN THIS STORY. BUT...HAS A "PACKAGE."

KOMACHI HIKIGAYA

HACHIMAN'S LITTLE SISTER. IN MIDDLE SCHOOL. EVERYTHING SHE DOES IS CALCULATED!?

HAYATO HAYAMA

TOP RANKED IN THE SCHOOL CASTE. HANDSOME MEMBER OF THE SOCCER TEAM.

YUMIKO MIURA

THE HIGH EMPRESS NONE CAN OPPOSE.

HINA EBINA

A MEMBER OF MIURA'S CLIQUE BUT A RAGING FUJOSHI ON THE INSIDE.

KAKERU TOBE

ALWAYS OVEREXCITED. MEMBER OF HAYAMA'S CLIQUE.

HARUNO YUKINOSHITA

YUKINO'S SISTER. UNIVERSITY UNDERGRADUATE. IS QUITE INTERESTED IN HACHIMAN.

SHIZUKA HIRATSUKA

GUIDANCE COUNSELOR. ATTEMPTING TO FIX HACHIMAN BY FORCING HIM INTO THE SERVICE CLUB.

SO FAR

EVERYONE IS WORKING TOWARD HOLDING A SOUBU HIGH PROM, WITH YUKINO AND IROHA IN CHARGE. BUT WHEN YUKINO'S MOTHER SUDDENLY TURNS UP AND INSISTS IT SHOULD BE CANCELED, THE PLANNING COMES TO A STANDSTILL. SEEING HOW THE GIRLS WANT THE EVENT TO PROCEED NO MATTER WHAT, HACHIMAN DECLARES HE'LL COME UP WITH A NEW PLAN — IN OTHER WORLDS, HE'LL RUN THE OPPOSITION. IT REMINDS HIM OF THE CONTEST THE SERVICE CLUB ONCE HELD WHERE THE WINNER MADE THE OTHERS DO WHATEVER THEY SAID...

CONTENTS

CHAPTER 97 ··· ONCE AGAIN, HACHIMAN HIKIGAYA MAKES A SPEECH. (Part One) → 001

CHAPTER 98 ··· ONCE AGAIN, HACHIMAN HIKIGAYA MAKES A SPEECH. (Part Two) → 031

CHAPTER 99 ··· AT SOME UNKNOWN POINT, THE ENDING CREDITS BEGIN TO ROLL. → 057

CHAPTER 100 ··· PRIVATELY, HAYATO HAYAMA FEELS REGRET. → 087

CHAPTER 100.5 ··· INTERLUDE HAYATO HAYAMA. → 119

CHAPTER 101 ··· WHAT HINA EBINA SEES THROUGH THE LENS IS... → 129

SPOT THE DIFFERENCES ANSWERS. → 162

NO, WAIT. HOLD UP.
IT'S NOT JUST ME. LOOK— YUKINOSHITA WAS BEING THAT WAY TOO, SO.....
YOU'RE TOTALLY OVERCOMPLICATING THINGS.
WHAT DO YOU MEAN, "I'VE THOUGHT ABOUT HOW I SHOULD SAY IT"?
LOOK— WHEN YOU'RE THAT STUBBORN AND THAT MUCH TROUBLE ...
UH-HUH. THANKS FOR INTRODUCING YOURSELF.
WAIT— I DON'T MEAN ME.
BUT ALSO ME.
NO PROB...

THIS IS THE ONLY WAY FOR US, IN THE END...
OR, LIKE, THIS IS THE ONLY WAY I KNOW, SO.....

SO.....I'M GRATEFUL TO YOU.
WE HAVE TO DRAW A LINE SOMEWHERE, OR WE'D HAVE KEPT ON DRAGGING THINGS OUT.
WE NEEDED A GOAL OR, LIKE, AN END POINT.

YOU'RE REALLY ALL...
...SO MUCH TROU-BLE...
SENPAI.
MM.

WHY AM I PICKING BETWEEN THESE TWO...?

CEORCIA
MAX COFFEE
練乳入り
WITH CONDENSED MILK • COFFEE BEVERAGE
コーヒー飲料

ぜんざい
つぶしぜんざい
RED BEAN SOUP CREAMY

ARE YOU ACTUALLY THAT FIXATED ON THE PROM?
...HEY.
UH, SINCE YOU NEVER REALLY WENT IN-DEPTH ABOUT IT.....
WHERE'S THIS COMING FROM .....?
I SUPPOSE IT'S REALLY, YOU KNOW, 'COS THERE WAS THE ISSUE OF HIRATSUKA-SENSEI LEAVING.
IS THAT ...?
THAT'S HOW IT GOES WITH WORK.
SORRY I COULDN'T SAY IT.
I GUESS SO...

.....YOU KNEW ABOUT THAT BEFORE?
YEAH, BASI-CALLY.
I'M DOING THE FAREWELL ADDRESS, RIGHT? SO I OVERHEARD IT THEN.

YOU CARE ABOUT HER THAT MUCH...
SOB...
OH, UH, WELL...

I WOULDN'T GO THAT FAR.
.....BUT IT'S FEASIBLE THAT MAYBE YOU COULD!
HUH? WHAT? WHAT WAS THAT?

SO I WAS THINK-ING, YOU KNOW?
WE HAVE TO GIVE HER A PROPER SEND-OFF AND A PROPER GOOD-BYE...
...OR IT FEELS LIKE WE'LL REGRET IT.

URK.
I MEAN, I FIGURE YOU'D BE LIKE, "I COULDN'T DO AAANYTHING" AND THEN REGRET IT HARD AFTER.
BUT YOU'RE THAT TYPE, AREN'T YOU, SENPAI?
I'M PROBABLY THAT TYPE TOO.

YUKINO-SENPAI AND YUI-SENPAI...

...AND HAYAMA-SENPAI...AND MIGHT AS WELL TOSS IN TOBE-SENPAI AND WHOEVER ELSE WHILE WE'RE AT IT.

I WANT TO SEND ALL YOU GUYS OFF RIGHT...

...
WELL, IT'S NOT LIKE I DON'T GET IT.
REEEALLY?
AHA, SO YOU'RE ACTUALLY A GOOD PERSON, EH?
IT'S SO I WON'T HAVE REGRETS, OKAY?
I'M DOING IT FOR MYSELF.
...THAT'S WHY I WANT TO HAVE THIS PROM.
SURU (SLIDE)
する
SU (SWF)
する
SO THEN...

SHAPE UP, PLEASE.
KYU (SQUEEZE)
きゅっ。
IF YOU DON'T, THEN I WON'T BE ABLE TO EITHER.

ぽん
PON
(PAT)
YEAH.
I'LL HANDLE IT.

...I STILL HAVE NO IDEA WHAT, SPECIFICALLY, I'M GONNA DO FOR IT.
THOUGH I SAID I'D MAKE THIS PROM HAPPEN ...

THOUGH THEIR CHOICE TO DEAL WITH THE SYMP-TOMS OF THE PROBLEM WASN'T A MISTAKE...

...IT LACKED FINAL-ITY.

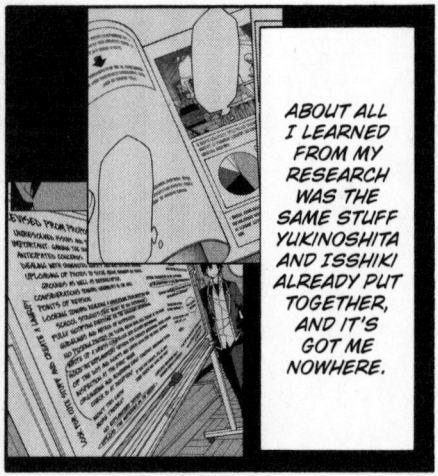
ABOUT ALL I LEARNED FROM MY RESEARCH WAS THE SAME STUFF YUKINOSHITA AND ISSHIKI ALREADY PUT TOGETHER, AND IT'S GOT ME NOWHERE.

"SHAPE UP, PLEASE."
I HAVE TO THINK UP SOME OTHER APPROACH .....
..... ANY-WAY—

OHH ...
LUNCH, HIKKI?
Y-YEAH.
YOU ATE?
UH-HUH.
OH.
...WERE YOU OKAY YESTER-DAY?
HUH?
TSU (STREAK)

OH...
AHH, YEAH. I'M TOTALLY OKAY!
OR LIKE I SAID BEFORE ...
...IT'S A COMMON THING, Y'KNOW?
...
...MIND IF I SIT... WITH YOU?

WELL, LOTS HAP-PENED.
I'VE DECIDED TO TRY TO MAKE THE PROM HAPPEN.
...OH.

YOU'RE HELPING YUKINON, RIGHT?
...
WELL, ABOUT THAT...

SANDWICH: BLUEBERRY SANDWICH
SO... YOU CAN LEAVE WITHOUT ME TODAY.
YEAH, I KNOW.

...HUH?

...IT'S LESS "HELPING" AND MORE LIKE "OPPOSING."
UH-HUH.

...UHH... HUH.
SO I'VE DECIDED TO COMPETE AGAINST HER.
NO, NOT LIKE THAT ...
SHE'S KINDA BEING REALLY STUBBORN ABOUT THIS, OKAY? THERE'S NO CHANCE IN HELL WE CAN WORK TOGETHER.
YOU GOT IT BACKWARD. I'M SOMETIMES REALLY SMART.
LIKE...YOU'RE SOMETIMES REALLY DUMB, HIKKI...
GUESS NOT...
...WOULD TALKING RESOLVE IT?
DID YOU ACTUALLY TALK WITH HER?

MUNGU CMUNCHO
むんむ
...I'M GONNA DEVISE ...
...ANOTHER PROM PLAN DIFFERENT FROM THEIRS.
SO THEN WHAT ARE YOU GONNA DO NOW?
HMM ...
WELL, I REALLY MULLED IT OVER...
SINCE THE PLAN'S BEEN SHOT DOWN ONCE, I THINK OUR ODDS OF JUST TRYING TO PUSH THE PROM THROUGH ARE BAD.
SO ...
RIGHT NOW, THE PARENTS ARE THINKING OF PROMS, IN GENERAL, AS BAD, SO WE HAVE TO COME UP WITH SOMETHING EVEN WORSE TO PUSH A NEW 'BIAS.'
...AND A FACT T ISSUES SU AS DRINKING AND IMPROPER SEXUAL CONDUCT DO OCCUR.
AND WHEN PROBLEMS DO CROP UP, YOU WON'T BE ABLE TO TAKE RESPONSI-BILITY FOR IT.
.....WHY?

SO YOU SHOULDN'T EAT TOO MUCH SWEETS, RIGHT?
Y-YEAH? WHY ARE YOU ...?
... SUGAR MAKES YOU FAT.
ムッ
...
I... SEE?
?
?
BUYERS?
THAT'S NOT WHAT I MEAN... BUT WELL, SURE.
YEAH, I COULD EAT TWO ...
...IF A NEW HALF-CALORIE ICE CREAM POPS UP, THEN YOU'D FEEL LIKE IT'S OKAY TO EAT THAT, RIGHT?
BUT THEN ...
THE STRATEGY IS TO PUT FORWARD A FAKE PLAN—A TRASH PROPOSAL—TO GET THE REAL ONE THROUGH.
BY MAKING IT A CHOICE BETWEEN TWO OPTIONS, WE MAKE THE PARENTS FEEL LIKE THEY HAVE TO CHOOSE ONE.
OHH, YOU MEAN THE PROM YUKINON AND IROHA-CHAN ARE WORKING ON IS THE HALF-CALORIE, HUH.

THAT'S EXACTLY THE THING ...
AH, BUT WHAT IF THEY SAY BOTH ARE NO GOOD?
THE SCHOOL DOESN'T REALLY WANT THE PROM TOTALLY CANCELED EITHER.
IF THEY DID, THEY WOULDN'T HAVE USED THE TERM SELF-RESTRAINT.
THE SCHOOL RESPECTS THE STUDENTS' AUTONOMY, SO KILLING IT NOW WOULD BE BAD FOR THEIR REPUTATION.
THAT'S TRUE... WE'VE PUT ON A LOT OF EVENTS BEFORE.....
...BUT THAT'S PROBABLY OKAY.
SO THE ODDS ARE HIGH THAT THE SCHOOL ADMINISTRATION WILL BE ON THE SIDE OF THE MORE REASONABLE OPTION.
MERRY CHRISTMAS!

THAT'S WHAT I FIGURE ANYWAY.
IT MEETS OUR STANDARDS!
APPROVED
AND THAT SHOWS THE PARENTS THAT WE'VE MADE COMPROMISES FOR THEM, WHILE ALSO MAKING IT SO IT'S LIKE THEY GOT TO CHOOSE AND ARE THE ONES WHO MADE THE DECISION. SO THAT SATISFIES THEM, AND THEY BACK OFF...
WELL ...
THERE'S A MAJOR OBSTACLE IN THIS PLAN.
YOU CAME UP WITH THIS IN ONE NIGHT, HIKKI?
THAT'S KINDA AMAZ-ING...
OH YEAH. IF WE DON'T, THEY'LL SEE THROUGH IT RIGHT AWAY...
AND IT HAS TO LOOK PRETTY LEGIT.
AHH ...
...WE HAVE TO PUT ACTUAL WORK INTO THIS SHAM PROPOSAL.

ACTUALLY, IT'S MORE LIKE, WHAT DO WE EVEN HAVE TO WORK WITH...?
AND NO FUNDS EITHER.
AND FOR THAT, WE DON'T HAVE ENOUGH TIME OR PEOPLE AT ALL.

YEAH, THAT'S THE ISSUE...
BUT WAIT. WOULD ANYONE EVEN BOTHER HELPING WITH A PLAN THAT'LL NEVER GET PASSED?

.....NO.
THAT WON'T CHANGE ANYTHING.
I GUESS I WHEEDLE AND CAJOLE AROUND TO GATHER AS MANY PEOPLE AS I CAN—

...GUESS I'LL TRY TALKING TO PEOPLE FOR REAL.
I DOUBT THEY'LL UNDERSTAND...
...BUT I'LL CALL UP SOME FOLKS WHO SEEM MOST LIKELY TO LISTEN.

—THAT...
.....I REALLY DON'T GET IT.
...WILL HELP YUKI-NON, RIGHT?
BUT...
...PROB-ABLY.
I HOPE SO...
SO I...
YEAH. THIS IS WHAT THEY'RE LIKE.

SO THEN...
...KEEP ON JUST A LITTLE MORE.
I'LL...
..... IS IT...
...SOMETHING I'M NOT ALLOWED TO HELP YOU WITH?
...WON'T COME TO AN END SO EASILY.
OUR STORY...

*ANSWERS ON PAGE 162

UNDER YUKINOSHITA'S LEADERSHIP, THE PREPARATIONS FOR THE SOUBU HIGH PROM WERE STEADILY ADVANCING...
THIS REALLY REALLY SUCKS.
SIGH
SOUBU HIGH PROM PLANNING COMMITTEE
SOUBU HIGH PROM PLANNING COMMITTEE
SOUBU HIGH PROM PLANNING COMMITTEE

WHAT WITH THAT FINAL REQUEST YUKINOSHITA MADE OF ME THAT SNOWY DAY..
I WOULD LIKE YOU BOTH TO BE WITNESSES TO WHAT I DO.
AND ITS CONCLUSION.
I WON'T HELP YOU.
...I WASN'T ABLE TO INVOLVE MYSELF WITH HER VERY WELL, BUT.....

WHAT ARE YOU TALKING ABOUT?
WHAT HAVE YOU ALL BEEN DOING, ALL THIS TIME?
THERE REALLY IS ONLY ONE WAY...
...FOR THE TWO OF US TO BE INVOLVED.

.....BUT I'M NOT SAYING I WON'T OPPOSE YOU.

"BUT I'LL CALL UP SOME FOLKS WHO SEEM MOST LIKELY TO LISTEN."
AND SO, TO GIVE YUIGAHAMA AND ME TIME TO COME UP WITH A FAKE PROM PROPOSAL TO PIT AGAINST YUKINOSHITA'S, WE STARTED GATHERING PEOPLE.
—SO.
PEOPLE WHO SEEM LIKE THEY'LL LISTEN...
SAIZERUYA
...MEANS THIS?
HRM?

HISO ひそ
I mean, what choice do we have?
There aren't many people I can work to the bone for no pay...
HISO ひそ (WHISPER)
...
Well, this is you, after all...
HEY, WHAT'S THAT SUPPOSED TO MEAN?

.....SO, HACHIMAN, WHAT IS THE MEANING OF THIS SUMMONS?
HMM? AHH, WELL, UHH...
...FOR NOW, JUST SPOT THE DIFFERENCES.
MM!
...THIS IS HARD, HUH.

AH!
LOOKS LIKE THEY JUST GOT HERE.
... WHO?
SORRY TO MAKE YOU WAIT, YUIGAHAMA-SAN!

HMM... TOTSUKA IS A RATHER DISCERNING PICK...
I ACTUALLY ASSUMED YOU INVITED HIM, THOUGH...
AND...
OH, HACHIMAN'S WITH YOU, AFTER ALL!

...DIDN'T I SAY PEOPLE WHO SEEMED LIKE THEY'D LISTEN?
YOU'RE THE ONE WHO INVITED M-2 SYNDROME!
I CAN HEAR YOU.

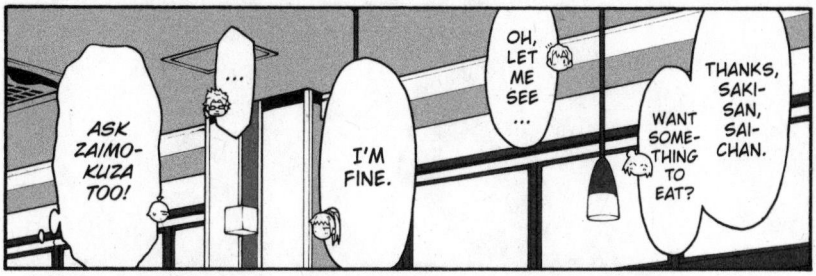
THANKS, SAKI-SAN, SAI-CHAN.
WANT SOMETHING TO EAT?
OH, LET ME SEE ...
I'M FINE.
...
ASK ZAIMOKUZA TOO!

...ALL RIGHT ...

ぺこり。
PEKORI (BOW)
FIRST, SORRY FOR CALLING YOU OUT HERE SO SUDDENLY. THANKS FOR COMING.
I APPRECIATE IT.
SO I HAVE SOME UNFORTUNATE NEWS.
OH-HO...
DO YOU GUYS KNOW WHAT A PROM IS?
NAY, I DO NOT.
SHU! (SWIPE)
THEREFORE, I WILL NOW GAIN THE KNOWLEDGE.
HNAAAAAAAAH!!?
SHUT UP.

DAN (BAND)
googlo
WHAT SORT OF FIENDISH EVENT IS THIS, TO EXIST PURELY TO FULFILL THE DESIRES FOR RECOGNITION AND TRANSITORY HEDONISM OF EXTROVERTED TYPES!?
ALL WHO GLORIFY SUCH EVENTS WILL, GENERALLY, ONCE THEY REACH UNIVERSITY...
...SPREAD THE STORY IN SPECIAL-EVENT CLUBS THAT "MY HIGH SCHOOL HAD A PROM" IN ORDER TO FALSIFY THEIR PASTS AND MAKE IT SEEM AS IF THEY'D BEEN COOL AND OUTGOING SOCIAL BUTTERFLIES EVER SINCE HIGH SCHOOL...
THEY ALWAYS BECOME HISTORICAL REVISIONISTS!!!!
HUHH...
SO WHAT ABOUT PROMS?
AH, YEAH ...
MM-HMM!
...ARE YOU SATISFIED NOW?

HUH?
BUT WE'VE DECIDED TO OPPOSE THAT.
THEY'RE TRYING TO HOLD A PROM AT OUR SCHOOL...
OHH ...!
I SEE! SO YOU ARE ANTI-PROM, AFTER ALL!
(LIKES THAT)
THOUGH, EVEN SAYING THAT...
IN OTHER WORDS, WE'RE ANTI-PROM!
...WELL, NOT QUITE, BUT NOT FAR OFF.
PACHIN (CLAPPED)

HUH? WHY!?
THAT'S OUR HACHIMAN!
I KNEW IT!
H-HMM... W-WELL, IT WOULD MEAN THAT, I GUESS?
IT'S A HASSLE TO EXPLAIN IT IN A WAY THAT WON'T KILL ZAIMOKUZA'S MOTIVATION.
UHHH...
UH... IT'S JUST KINDA HARD TO SAY THAT.
WHAT'S THIS ABOUT? AREN'T WE DOING A PROM?
BUT IT'LL BE BAD IF YOU DON'T TELL THEM.
YEAH...
I'LL BE COUNTING ON YOU TO BACK ME UP IF SOMETHING HAPPENS.
PLEASE AND THANKS.
...AGH. GUESS I GOTTA.

SO NOW, I HAVE AN UNFORTUNATE ANNOUNCEMENT TO MAKE.
UMM—

WE'RE GONNA HAVE A PROM.
WE ARE INDEED IN OPPOSITION, BUT WE'RE NOT NECESSARILY ANTI-PROM.

UM...

?
PAR-DON?

YUKINON AND IROHA-CHAN ARE PLANNING A PROM, BUT THE PARENTS AND SCHOOL HAVE TOLD THEM THEY HAVE TO "EXERCISE SELF-RESTRAINT."

SO WE'RE KINDA COMING UP WITH A WHOLE OTHER PLAN.

NO, I HAVEN'T TOLD HER. SORRY, BUT PLEASE DON'T TELL ANYONE.
IF PEOPLE FIND OUT WHAT WE'RE AFTER, THERE'LL BE NO POINT.
HRM. SUGGESTING A FALSE PREMISE...
A DOUBLE BIND.
YEAH, THAT'S BASICALLY OUR INTENTION.
DOUBLE BIND?
IT REFERS TO A PSYCHOLOGICAL TECHNIQUE WHERE, BY PRESENTING TWO OPTIONS, YOU PREEMPTIVELY KEEP THEM FROM CHOOSING THE OPTION OF NEITHER.

IT MEANS THEIRS IS THE HALF-CALORIE!
HALF-CALORIE ...?
UH... YOU DON'T HAVE TO BRING THAT UP.
SO I'D LIKE YOU GUYS TO HELP ME THINK ABOUT THAT NEW PROM...
HACHI-MAN—
WHAT DO YOU WANT TO DO?

YOU DIDN'T SEEM LIKE YOU WERE REALLY INTO THE PROM, JUST NOW.
SO I WONDERED IF MAYBE YOU WANTED TO DO SOMETHING ELSE.
KONEX
I MEAN, WELL...
SORRY. I'LL HEAR YOU OUT, HACHIMAN.
IF I DON'T, I THINK I WON'T REALLY GET THINGS IN THE END, JUST LIKE ALWAYS, AND I KIND OF DON'T WANT THAT...

I ALWAYS WISHED I HAD SUPPORT FROM THEM LIKE THIS.
THE BIG PLAN TO KEEP YUKINO-SAN AND YUI-SAN IN THE CLUB!?
I'M GOING TO NEGOTIATE WITH EROU!
BEFORE, I HID EVERYTHING AND BORROWED REASONS FROM OTHERS. I WAS JUST DEPENDING ON THEIR KINDNESS.
BUT NOW, THINGS ARE DIFFER-ENT.
HIKKI ...

—TO BE FRANK...

...I DON'T CARE MUCH ABOUT THE PROM ITSELF.

EVEN IF IT'S PATHETIC AND SPINELESS...

...AT THE VERY LEAST, I'LL SPEAK NO LIES.

I WANT TO MAKE THEIR PROM HAPPEN...
...IS WHAT I THINK.

THE PROPOSAL I'M TRYING TO PUT TOGETHER IS WHAT YOU'D CALL A THROWAWAY.
IT'S FABRICATED FOR THE SAKE OF GETTING THROUGH WHAT WE REALLY WANT.
SO KNOWING THAT IT'LL BE FOR NOTHING...
...IF YOU'RE STILL OKAY WITH THAT...
...THEN HELP ME OUT.

……THANKS.
I HAVE MY CLUB ACTIVITIES, SO I CAN'T HELP WITH EVERYTHING …
…BUT LET ME KNOW IF YOU NEED SOME EXTRA HANDS. I'LL BRING THE WHOLE TENNIS CLUB TO PITCH IN.
THANKS. I'LL BE COUNTING ON YOU.

...SORRY.
I'M HELPING YUKINOSHITA ...
...SO I CAN'T GO HALF-IN ON THAT. I HAVE TO DO IT PROPERLY.
NO, IT'S ACTUALLY GREAT IF YOU COULD HELP THEM.
SINCE THAT ONE'S THE REAL DEAL.

THANKS.
I DON'T NEED TO HEAR THAT FROM YOU.
.....BUT GOOD LUCK.

SU (SLIDE)

HRRM ...

—WELL, OUR ONLY COURSE OF ACTION IS FOR IT TO BE DONE.
BUTSU (MUTTER)
...AROUND THIS TIME, PROBABLY THE NISHI-CHIBA LUCKY. OR NO, MAYBE NUMA ACE.
BUTSU
ZA (STRIDE)
UM, ZAIMO-KUZA-SAN...?
YOU HAVE NEED OF MEN, RIGHT?
MAKE SOME TIME ON THE MORROW.
I'LL SEND WORD.

BASA (FLAP)
BA (FWIP)
WAIT!
AND HOPE!!
HAA HA HA HA HA!

M-2 SEEMS KINDA FULL OF CONFIDENCE...
DOES HE HAVE SOME CONNEC-TIONS OR SOMETHING .....?
WHO KNOWS ...?
HOP
LOCKMFST

WHOA, I JUST GOT A DM FROM SWORDS-MAN-SAN...
WHAT? ON DISBOARD?
NO, TWEETER.
HUH? FOR REAL .....?
I GOT A REAL BAD FEELING ABOUT THIS.
FOR SURE ...

CHAPTER 99 ··· AT SOME UNKNOWN POINT, THE ENDING CREDITS BEGIN TO ROLL.

CHAPTER 99 ··· AT SOME UNKNOWN POINT, THE ENDING CREDITS BEGIN TO ROLL.

HI...
...IT'S BEEN A LONG TIME.
TH-THANKS ...
KASA (RUSTLE)
TON (TUP)
THE U.G. CLUB.
HEY. THIS IS THE U.G. CLUB... RIGHT?
YEAH ...

I REMEMBER THAT BEFORE, ON A REQUEST FROM ZAIMOKUZA, WE PLAYED MILLIONAIRE AGAINST THESE GUYS.
MILLION-AIRE, RIGHT?
YES! THIS IS SUPER FUN!!
...AND TWEAK IT A LITTLE.
OH, I WAS HERE TO PLAY THIS!!
I MEAN, 'COS IF WE LOSE, WE HAVE TO STRIP.
PLAY-TIME IS OVER.
ZAIMO-KUZA, SO THE HELP YOU MEN-TIONED...
"YOU HAVE NEED OF MEN, RIGHT.
"MAKE SOME TIME ON THE MORROW."
DOOON (BAAN)
AYE!
...
HATANO-SHI AND SAGAMI-SHI!!

WHICH IS WHICH ...?
I CAN'T TELL THEM APART...
Seriously, I thought for sure there was no way...
HISO
HISO. (WHISPER) D.O.O.
Whoa, Swordsman-san was totally right.

GUESS I'LL TAKE THESE GUYS SERI-OUSLY THIS TIME.
BESIDES, IT'S A FACT WE NEED ALL THE HELP WE CAN GET...
NO THANKS
BUT ZAIMOKUZA OF ALL PEOPLE REACHED OUT TO SOME GUYS NOT ONLY YOUNGER THAN HIM BUT WHO MADE A FOOL OUT OF HIM, TO BOOT.

UM...SO I'M SURE YOU'VE HEARD THIS ALREADY ...
...BUT IN ORDER TO PUSH THROUGH THE STUDENT COUNCIL'S PROM...
...WE'RE GONNA TO HAVE YOU HELP US PUT TOGETHER A DECOY SCHEME THAT DELIBERATELY OPPOSES IT.

I CAN HEAR YOU.
Is he out of his mind...?
Organizing something so big just for that...
HISO
HISO (WHISPER)
He's got to be brain-dead.

N-NGH...
HIKKI, YOU HAVE TO ACTUALLY TALK TO THEM.

...THIS IS GONNA SOUND BAD...

HIS METHODS ARE ALWAYS AS STRANGELY INSCRUTABLE AS THUS!
RIGHT? THIS IS HACHIMAN HIKIGAYA!
JACK-ASS...
PUPU (PFFFT)

EVEN A POLITICIAN WOULD CHOOSE HIS WORDS SLIGHTLY BETTER...
THAT REALLY DOES SOUND BAD...
PLEASE JUST THINK OF YOURSELVES AS OLYMPIC VOLUNTEERS, RESIGN YOURSELVES, AND HELP US OUT.
...BUT WE NEED YOU AS FREE LABOR WE CAN USE AS MUCH AS WE WANT.

S-SORRY.
HIKKI'S JUST KINDA LIKE, YOU KNOW.....
HM.
HN.
THAT ISN'T A DEFENSE ...
...
...WHAT DO WE DO?
HMMGH, I SAY NAY.
YOU'RE AGAINST THIS...?
UM.....
I DON'T WANT TO GO TO THIS "PROM" THING IN THE FIRST PLACE.....

...THE TRUTH IS, JUST BETWEEN US...
BUT I CAN'T BACK OUT ON THIS ONE.
...WELL, YEAH, OF COURSE.
I GET THAT.
UH-HUH ...?
...?
...THEY'VE DEMANDED THE PROM ORGANIZERS EXERCISE SELF-RESTRAINT.
UH, LIKE WE SAID, WE CAN JUST NOT GO...
...IT'S JUST SELF-SE-STRAINT, RIGHT?
FOR THE FROM...
I JUST HEARD SOMEONE ELSE SAYING SOMETHING VERY SIMILAR.
... ACTUALLY, THERE'S ABOUT AN EIGHTY PERCENT CHANCE IT'LL HAPPEN ANYWAY.
BUT PUT ANOTHER WAY, SELF-RESTRAINT IS THE ONLY CAVEAT. THEY COULD JUST GO THROUGH WITH IT.

JUST IMAGINE IT...
SUPPOSE YOU DON'T GO TO THE PROM NOW. THAT'LL MOST LIKELY MAKE IT DIFFICULT TO SHOW YOUR FACES AT THE COMING-OF-AGE CEREMONY AND ALUMNI EVENTS.
BUT HOLD ON.
YOU'RE WEARING THE SUIT YOUR FATHER BOUGHT YOU THE OTHER DAY WHEN YOU WENT SHOPPING TOGETHER FOR THE FIRST TIME IN YEARS...
HE'S GOING INTO SOME-THING...
IT'S THE MORNING OF THE COMING-OF-AGE CEREMONY.
HERE.
WAIT, HONEY.
DAD
MOM
GOSO (RUSTLE)

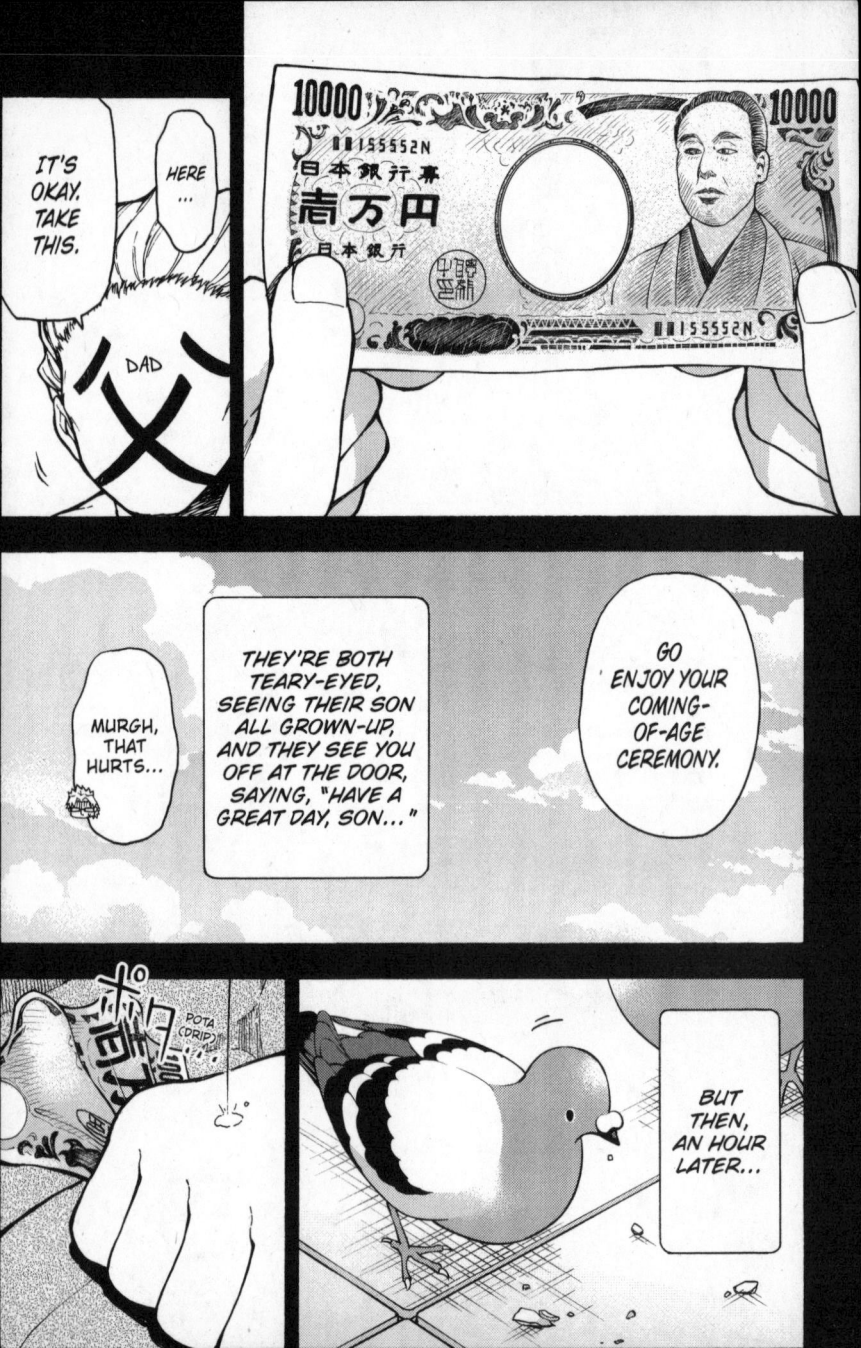
IT'S OKAY. TAKE THIS.
HERE ...
DAD
10000
10000
日本銀行
壱万円
日本銀行
GO ENJOY YOUR COMING-OF-AGE CEREMONY.
THEY'RE BOTH TEARY-EYED, SEEING THEIR SON ALL GROWN-UP, AND THEY SEE YOU OFF AT THE DOOR, SAYING, "HAVE A GREAT DAY, SON..."
MURGH, THAT HURTS...
POTA (DRIP)
BUT THEN, AN HOUR LATER...

SORRY, MOM, DAD...
I COULDN'T GO TO THE CEREMONY...
THEN AFTER THAT, YOU GO TO THE ARCADE TO BLOW YOUR MONEY, BINGE ICE CREAM AT A NET CAFÉ, AND ONCE YOUR STOMACH'S COOLED DOWN, YOU JUST KEEP DRINKING MISO SOUP TO KILL TIME...
NGH ...
HOW TRAGIC ...
AND THAT NIGHT, WHEN YOU SNEAK BACK HOME...
SO THERE'S MORE ...
THE LIGHTS ARE OUT, BUT YOUR PARENTS DELIB-ERATELY STAYED AWAKE.
...DID YOU HAVE FUN?
W-WELL, IT WAS NORMAL .....
DAD
MOM

ほろり…
HORORI (MOVED)
MOM
...YOU'RE ALL GROWN-UP ALREADY, YOSHITERU.
ME!?
THIS IS ME!?
BUT A PROM THAT'S TOO BIG AND LOUD WILL BE TOO HIGH A HURDLE!
SO WE MAKE ONE THAT'S AT LEAST A LITTLE QUIETER TO BUILD OUR EXPERIENCE POINTS!
SO AS TO NOT WIND UP LIKE THAT!
WE MUST GIRD OUR-SELVES!
WITH THE GUILE TO ENDURE THESE EVENTS!!
GATA (SLAM)
ざわっ
ZAWA (UNEASE)

SO WORK WITH US TO INSURE THEIR PROM GOES THROUGH.
I WOULDN'T CALL THIS A REWARD...
...BUT WE'LL USE OUR INFLUENCE TO GUARANTEE YOUR OPINIONS WILL BE REFLECTED IN FUTURE PROMS AFTER THIS ONE.
...
HRM?
HUH?
I'M OKAY WITH IT.
...SO THEN...

WELL, I'D KINDA LIKE TO AVOID ANY FAMILIAL SHAME BEFORE IT HAPPENS...
?
MY BIG SISTER IS THE TYPE TO ALWAYS BUTT IN OVER THINGS LIKE THAT.
...SO I'D LIKE TO PROACTIVELY MAKE SURE THAT DOESN'T COME TO PASS.
SAGAMI .....

SAGAMI!...?

...?

HAVEN'T I HEARD THAT NAME SOME-WHERE ...?
...THAT SHE'S NOT HELPING ANYONE OR ANY-THING?
JUST STOP TALKING.
SHUT UP.

AH.
SAGAMI— SO YOU'RE THAT ONE'S LITTLE BROTHER?
OHH.
THAT ONE
AHH.
URK ...!
FOR REAL?
...BUT IT'D IRRITATE ME TO FEEL ASHAMED AT GRADUATION ...
SO FINE. I'LL HELP.
...
I HONESTLY DON'T REALLY CARE...

.....SO CAN WE LEAVE IT TO TOMORROW TO GET STARTED?
FIRST, WE'LL PULL TOGETHER WHATEVER MATERIALS WE CAN ON OUR END.
O-OKAY...

ALL RIGHT, THEN IF THAT'S IT...
YEAH. SEE YOU GUYS TOMORROW.
?

HUH? NO HANG-OUT NOW? WHAT ABOUT THE ICEBREAKER !?
HUH ...?
UH, WE'RE NOT DOING THAT...
WE DON'T HAVE TIME ANYWAY.

UHHHH?
ISN'T IT GREAT WE GOT THEIR HELP?
YEAH.

OF COURSE...
O-OH...
I'LL GET A JUMP ON THE WORK NOW...
...SINCE I AM MORE OR LESS THE PROJECT LEADER.
THINGS'LL GET BUSY STARTING TOMORROW.

I'M GONNA HELP, OKAY !?
HUH? UH, I CAN DO IT ALONE...
I-I'LL HELP TOO!
TATSUYA

NOT JUST WITH THE PROM BUT LOTS OF OTHER STUFF TOO...

I DON'T WANT TO MAKE YOU SHOULDER EVERYTHING ...

...GOT IT.
SIGN: LIVING CLUB
生活CLUB
24h
生活CLU
OHH...

WHY PAIR SEATING...?
I—I MEAN—!
THIS WAS THE ONLY ONE OPEN!!
WE CAN WORK HERE, SO DON'T COMPLAIN!!
WELL...
SHE SAYS THAT, BUT...

SHE'S TOO CLOSE ...
WH-WHAT'S WITH THAT LOOK!!?

ABOUT WHAT?
HEY, WHAT DO WE DO?
KATA (CLACK)
KATA
19:36
VENUE.
OUR SCHOOL DOESN'T HAVE A DANCE HALL SORT OF PLACE LIKE IN THIS MOVIE.
YUKINOSHITA AND THE OTHERS ARE PLANNING TO USE THE GYM, SO I'D LIKE TO PROPOSE SOMETHING ELSE, IF POSSIBLE...
WE COULD DO IT OUTSIDE THE SCHOOL.
IT'S NOT LIKE A PROM HAS TO BE IN A SPECIFIC PLACE, RIGHT?
OH, THEN DESTINY—
NOT REALISTIC, BUDGET-WISE.

WHERE?
THEN HOW ABOUT THE BEACH?
HMM...
MUUU (POUT)
I JUST WANTED TO TRY SAYING IT.

THAT'S TOKYO BAY.....
IT'D BE EASY TO TAKE PROMO PHOTOS TOO.
THE ONE REAL CLOSE TO THE SCHOOL.

AND THEN...
WHEN YOU SEE THAT, IT MAKES YOU FEEL, LIKE, "I HAD ANOTHER FUN DAY TODAY."
AND THEN, LIKE, IN THE EVENINGS, THE SUN ALWAYS SETS INTO THE SEA...

...IS WHAT YOU FEEL.
..."I WISH THESE DAYS COULD GO ON FOR EVER".....

GRATEFUL SCHOOL
グレイトフルスクール
アメリカンプロ
AMERICAN PRO
…YEAH.

TOKUN
TOKUN
TOKUN (PADUMO)
TOKUN

HIKKI...
.....I'M GONNA LIE DOWN FOR A BIT.
...OKAY.

BEFORE I KNEW IT...

...THINGS ARE HEADING TOWARD AN INEVITABLE END.

WHATEVER I CHOOSE...

I DIDN'T HAVE TIME TO WONDER, AS THE CREDITS BEGAN TO ROLL.

HEYLOOO!
WH-WHAT'S "HEYLO" ...?
WHOA, SHE REALLY IS A LOT...
...DON'T WORRY ABOUT THAT.
WE'VE GOT SOMETHING MORE IMPORTANT TO TALK ABOUT.
(CREAK)

HENCE-FORTH, GREETINGS DURING ALL COMMITTEE MEETINGS WILL BE STANDARD-IZED AS "HEYLO."
HE'S AN IDIOT ...
H-HIKKI ...
HE'S GOTTA BE MESSED IN THE HEAD, AFTER ALL...
KAAAA (BLUUUUSH)
D-DON'T ...
IT'S GOTTEN EMBARRASSING NOW, SO LET'S STOP...
WELL THEN, ONCE AGAIN ...
AYE.
CHIKI (TK) チキ ...
HEYLO'S GOOD...
...NO, HEYLO IS GOOD.

HEYLOOO !!
STOP.

WELL, MOVING TO THE SUBJECT AT HAND...

PLAN ON WHAT TO DO FOR THE FAKE PROM
UHH, SO THE CONCEPT IS SOMETHING LOUDER AND MORE AUDACIOUS THAN THE LAST PROPOSAL...
LET'S GET THIS PLANNING MEETING STARTED.

...
OHH!
A CAMPFIRE!
THAT KINDA SEEMS LIKE SOME-THING MEMORA-BLE!

THAT'S AN IDEA.
OHH, OHH!
FIRE-WORKS!
I LIKE SEEING AND LIGHTING THEM!

MM, YEAH.
OHH!
A FOOD STALL!
I THINK THAT'S AN IDEA.

I MEAN ...
...YOU'RE JUST BRINGING UP ALL THE THINGS YOU DID OVER SUMMER VACATION.

...WHAT ARE YOU FORCING US TO WITNESS, YOU ASSHOLE?
TERE (BLUSH) ...
WHEN I'M TRYING TO THINK ABOUT STUFF THAT WAS FUN, THAT'S WHAT I WIND UP WITH...
TCH!

COS-PLAY... COULD WORK.
YOU'RE PROB-ABLY IMAG-INING SOME-THING ELSE .....
OH, LIKE HALLOWEEN?

SAGAMI.
THIS IS BASICALLY THE KINDA STUFF YOUR SISTER WOULD LIKE.
I DON'T WANNA THINK ABOUT IT...
WHIM

UM...
...IT DOESN'T QUITE SEEM RIGHT.
HMM...
FOOD STALL
FIREWORKS
CAMPFIRE
COSPLAY
SONGS
PLAY
ACCLAMATION

LET'S COME AT IT FROM A FRESH ANGLE.
...
YOURS GUYS' POINTS ARE WAY TOO REASON-ABLE...
IF NOBODY'S DOING SOMETHING, MAYBE YOU SHOULD CONSIDER WHY.
IS THERE EVEN A REASON TO FIRE RANDOM COUNTERS AT THE OTHER PROM IDEA?
KYU (SQUEAK)
ANTI-PARENTS
THIS IS IT.
AND TO THAT END...
...THE NUMBER ONE THING IS "REALISM."
THE FAKE PROM
FOOD STALL
FIREWORKS
CAMPFIRE
COSPLAY
SONGS
PLAY
ANTI-PARENTS
ANTI-PARENTS
WE SHOULD THINK ABOUT HOW WE CAN BEST BE DISCOVERED BY SOME OF THE PARENTS...
...AND THEN HOW WE CAN GET THEM TO STOP US.

NOPE.
HUHH…
CAN YOU DO SOMETHING LIKE THAT?
KYU
PARENTS
JOINT PROM EVENT WITH CHIBA KAIHIN AREA
EMENTARY/MIDDLE/HIGH SCH
AT THIS POINT, WHETHER WE CAN DO IT OR NOT ISN'T THE ISSUE. THE IMPORTANT THING IS MAKING THEM THINK WE'RE GOING TO.
FOR NOW, WE MAKE SOME "INQUIRIES" TO NEARBY SCHOOLS.
WE THEN PLANT THAT INFORMATION TO GET THE PARENTS WORRIED.
THEN WHAT ABOUT KAIHIN GENERAL?
WE WORKED WITH THEM BEFORE.
DEALING WITH THEM IS SO HARD, THOUGH …
SO THAT INFO… HAS GOT TO GET ONLINE, RIGHT?
I FIGURE.

WHOA, HE GOT THE EASY JOB...
I'LL FULLY COPY-PASTE OUT SOME-THING LOW-IQ!
LEAVE THE SOCIAL MEDIA TO ME!
FOR STARTERS, LET'S MAKE A SOCIAL MEDIA ACCOUNT AND A WEBSITE.

DIRECTOR YUIGAHAMA
SEEKING YOUR NAME SUGGESTIONS
AND THEN THERE'S THE GROUP NAME .....
GROUP NAME?
KYU (SQUEAK)
KYU
A HEART ...

MAKING A SITE, DOES THAT MEAN HTML?
WELL, IT'S FINE, THOUGH... PLEASE GIVE US A BIT OF TIME FOR RESEARCH.
A WEBSITE, HUH...

THESE GUYS MAY BE MORE COMPETENT THAN I THOUGHT ...
BUT WHAT DO WE DO ABOUT THE DOMAIN AND SERVER?
LET'S LOOK FOR SOME FREE SOFT-WARE
CAN'T WE JUST CHOOSE A TEMPLATE FROM A BUILDER?
I DUNNO. LET'S JUST GOOGLE IT.

HRM.
IF IT'S SOMETHING BESIDES THE STUDENT COUNCIL...
OH, LIKE THE CLUB CAPTAINS' ASSOCIATION.
WE OBVIOUSLY CAN'T CALL OURSELVES THE STUDENT COUNCIL TOO.
OR WE COULD PARASITE OFF SOME OTHER ORGANIZATION ...
ANTI-PARENTS
OHH, I DIDN'T KNOW THEY WERE THINKING ABOUT THAT.
KAIHIN GENERAL
...THE CAPTAINS' ASSOCIATION ISN'T SATISFIED WITH HOW THE PROM IS GOING...
...SO THEY'RE INDEPENDENTLY CONSIDERING A JOINT SEND-OFF PARTY AMONG ALL THE CLUBS.
...MAKE IT BIG ENOUGH, AND IT'S FUNCTIONALLY A PROM.
OH, NOT LIKE I KNOW.
HUH?

UN (NOD)
うんうん
UN
THIS GUY IS GREAT AT BULL-SHITTING .....
OH, THAT'S WHAT YOU MEAN BY MAKING IT LOOK REALISTIC TO PARENTS.

WHO'S IN CHARGE OF THE CAPTAINS' ASSOCIATION?
PLAN ON WHAT TO DO FOR THE
PROM
SOCIAL MEDIA ACCOUNT
ANTI-PARENTS
WEBSITE
OKAY, I CAN BASI-CALLY SEE IT NOW.

URK.
HAYATO-KUN.

WELL... I GUESS I HAVE TO JUST DEAL WITH THAT...
THEN LET'S LEAVE IT THERE FOR TODAY.
YOU GUYS HAN-DLE THE REST.
THANKS, GUYS!
YOU GOT IT.
YUP.
AYE !!
SIGH...
I DON'T WANNA DO THIS...
MY.

HIKIGAYA-KUN.
... HEY.
TAKING A BREAK ...?
YES.
I CAME TO GET SOME AIR.
SU (SWF)

...HOW ARE THINGS GOING?
IT'S UNUSUAL FOR YOU TO BE CONCERNED ABOUT SOMEONE ELSE.
THAT'S NOT TRUE.
OF COURSE I'M GONNA KEEP AN EYE ON ENEMY ACTIVITY.
KUSU (GIGGLE)
I'M JEALOUS ...
THINGS ARE GOING FAIRLY WELL.
WE HAVE A THOROUGH UNDERSTANDING OF THE TASKS AT HAND, AND WE'VE COORDINATED MATTERS WITH RELATED PARTIES.
...THERE'S NO NEED TO FORCE YOURSELF SO MUCH.
GOÒRCIO

...
...I'VE ALWAYS BEEN FORCING MYSELF.
THIS IS NORMAL FOR ME.
HUH?
...
I SEE ...
IN FACT ...

SUU
(SNOOZE)

WHICH ONE OF US IS FORCING THEMSELVES ...?
GOOD GRIEF...

KAAA (BLUSH)
あぁっ
AH!
...I'M SORRY.
HOW LONG WAS I ASLEEP?
NAH, IT WAS JUST A FEW MINUTES.
ウィーンウィーン...
WWV (BZZZZ)
AHAMA

AH...
...DID HAYAMA CONTACT YOU?
YEAH ...
...
...YUIGAHAMA-SAN. HELLO.
YEAH.
...HEYLO, YUKINON.
...I'LL RETURN TO WORK TOO.

WAIT.
YUKI-NON—
HAVE YOU BEEN AVOIDING ME?
...NOT AT ALL.
IT'S JUST WITH PREPARATIONS FOR THE PROM AND THE NOTICE OF CANCELLATION COMING UP, THERE'S BEEN A LOT TO DO...

UM, LISTEN ...

I'M HELPING HIKKI.

...IT'S ALL RIGHT. I DO UNDERSTAND.
...YOU DON'T GET IT.
I PLAN TO FOLLOW THROUGH. AND ONCE THIS IS OVER...I REALLY WILL FOLLOW THROUGH.
...SO YOU WON'T GET YOUR WISH, YUKINON.
...I SEE.
...I BELIEVE IT WOULD BE BEST IF YOUR OWN WISH CAME TRUE.
...DO YOU KNOW WHAT I REALLY WANT?
ARE YOU SURE ?
...YES, I THINK SO.
BECAUSE IT'S PROBABLY THE SAME.
THEN I'LL BE GOING...

KA (TAP)
AND I'LL GO SLEEP OVER AT YOUR PLACE AGAIN.
ONCE THE PROM'S OVER, WE'LL GO OUT TO EAT TOGETHER.

AND WE'LL GO TO DESTINY LAND AND DESTINY SEA DURING SPRING BREAK, AND THEN YOU'LL COME STAY OVER AT MY PLACE AGAIN...
AND THEN, IN APRIL...

WHAT SHOULD WE DO IN APRIL?
THERE'S SO MUCH STUFF I WANNA DO TOGETHER.
ENOUGH THAT IT'LL TAKE YEARS. DECADES, EVEN.
THAT..... REALLY IS A LOT.
CAN WE DO ALL THAT?
YEAH! BECAUSE I'LL STAY WITH YOU UNTIL WE DO IT ALL.

YOU GET THAT?
...SO IT'LL BE ALL RIGHT.
YES.
I DO.

.....I CAN'T UNDER-STAND IT, HONESTLY.
HUH?
THE CAPTAINS' ASSOCIATION WILL BE WORKING WITH THE STUDENT COUNCIL.
ACTUALLY, WE'RE PURELY UNDER THEIR CONTROL AS AN ORGANI-ZATION.
SO WE AREN'T ABLE TO HELP YOU.

...SO THEN, HOW ABOUT AS AN INDIVIDUAL?
I WANT THAT EVEN LESS.

I'LL OFFER MY FULL SUPPORT FOR THE REAL PROM...
...BUT I CAN'T COOPERATE WITH YOU AS A PART OF THE CAPTAINS' ASSOCIATION OR PERSONALLY.
...HOWEVER, I WON'T STOP OTHER CLUB MEMBERS FROM LENDING THEIR ASSISTANCE.
... THIS IS THE ONE CON-CESSION I CAN MAKE.

...WELL, I FIGURED YOU'D SAY AS MUCH.
THAT'LL DO.
...IT REMINDED ME OF THE PAST.
?
WHAT DID?

YOU KNOW SHE WAS ISOLATED IN ELEMENTARY SCHOOL?
SHE SAID SOMETHING SIMILAR BACK THEN TOO.
"I CAN DO IT MYSELF. I'M NOT RELYING ON YOU.
"I DON'T NEED YOUR HELP," SHE SAID.
...I'VE HEARD SOME-THING LIKE THAT BEFORE.
.....I WASN'T ABLE TO DO ANYTHING ABOUT IT.

I SHOULD HAVE DONE EVERYTHING I COULD TO HELP HER THEN. IF I HAD...
THAT'S YOUR OWN REGRETS TALKING.
DON'T SHOVE THEM OFF ON ME.
YOU CAN'T JUST BE ONE FOOT IN, ONE FOOT OUT ABOUT THIS.
YOU NEED TO TAKE THIS SERIOUSLY AND GIVE IT EVERYTHING YOU HAVE.
YEAH ...
STILL ...

I REALLY CAN'T STAND HOW HE GETS LIKE THIS.

I HONESTLY HATE IT.

THAT'S WHY I CAN SAY THIS TOO.

THE WAY YOU HANDLE THINGS IS WRONG, HIKIGAYA.

I DON'T THINK THAT'S WHAT YOU SHOULD BE DOING.

IF SHE DOESN'T NEED MY HELP...
...BUT I STILL WANT TO HELP HER ANYWAY...
...THEN THIS ISN'T CODEPEN-DENCY.
HIKIGAYA .....
DO YOU KNOW WHAT THAT FEELING IS CALLED?

I KNOW.
IT'S CALLED "A MAN'S PRIDE."

CHAPTER 100.5 ··· **INTERLUDE HAYATO HAYAMA.**

HAVE YOU FORGIVEN ME?

—SO ...
...I WANT YOU TO INCLUDE YUKINOSHITA-SAN.
I'VE REGRETTED IT EVER SINCE THAT DAY.
YUKINO-CHA—

"I DON'T NEED YOUR HELP."
IS SOME-THING WRONG ?
...NO.

SO YOU ACTUALLY SAID...
...
"CODEPEN-DENCY"?
OH WOW.
SO HE TALKS ABOUT THINGS LIKE THAT WITH YOU.
NO, HE JUST MENTIONED IT WHILE DISCUSSING SOMETHING ELSE.
.....BUT I CAN THINK OF SOMEONE WHO WOULD USE THAT KIND OF LANGUAGE TO PROVOKE HIM.
NOT BAD, ACE DETECTIVE.
BINGO.

I THINK FEELINGS CAN GROW OUT OF THAT TOO.

THEY WERE FINE LIKE THAT. GOING ABOUT IT BIT BY BIT...
THAT'S ALL JUST FAKE.
I ONLY WANT TO SEE SOME-THING REAL.

NEVER.

IT WAS NEVER LIKE THAT *BEFORE*, WAS IT?

IN ORDER TO KEEP WHAT SHE TREASURES FROM BEING FURTHER DAMAGED BY OTHERS, SHE'LL GET THE JUMP ON THEM AND SMASH IT HERSELF.

THIS IS A CURSE.
THIS IS LOVE.
NOT AT ALL.
THINKING, IF THEY JUST COULD...
SO I FORCED IT ON HIM.
I NEVER GOT MY CHANCE FOR ATONEMENT.
OH, I REALLY DO ENVY THEM.

IF YOU CAN NEED EACH OTHER AND FALL TO HELL TOGETHER, THERE'S NOTHING HAPPIER.
CAFFE &DINNER
BLUE SKY
CHIRIN (CLINK)
IF I'D HAD THAT IN MY GRASP...
...I'M SURE I WOULD HAVE BEEN ABLE TO GIVE THIS TWISTED SHAPE A NAME.
abidas

IF I HAD, THEN...
IF I'D GIVEN EVERYTHING I HAD TO SAVE HER THEN...
THAT'S WHY I STILL REGRET IT NOW.
...WOULD YOU HAVE FORGIVEN ME?

遊戯部
U.G. CLUB
遊戯部
U.G. CLUB
HUUUUH? THAT'S NOT CUTE!

HACHIMAN, I BROUGHT THE CAMERA YOU ASKED FOR.
AH, THANKS.
WELL, YOU KNOW, JUST, LIKE, MORE, LIKE, SPARKLE...
SPARKLE...?
...UMM, IF YOU COULD BE A BIT MORE SPECIFIC.
FOOD STALL
FIREWORKS
CAMPFIRE
COSPLAY
SONGS
PLAY
ACCLAMATION
LETTER TIME

I THOUGHT UP...A NAME...
TERE (BLUSH)
HUH?
FOR WHAT?

MOJI
MOJI (FIDGET)
もじもじ...

ALSO ...
Nikou

SOUBU HIGH SCHOOL NEO-PROM-JECT

YUIGAHAMA

SEEKING YOUR NAME SUGGESTIONS

NEGOTIATE WITH CAPTAINS' ASSOCIATION HAYAMA

AH...

A NAME, HUH.

PLAN ON WHAT TO D

SOCIAL MEDIA ACCOUNT ZAIMOKUZA

WEBSITE

ANTI-PARE

YEEK!

PLEASE LOOK FORWARD TO YOSHITERU ZAIMOKUZA-SENSEI'S NEXT CREATIVE WORK!

I THINK IT'S ACTUALLY A GOOD TITLE THAT'S SURE TO GO PLACES.

I SEE...

AHH, I BASICALLY GET IT, IT'S FINE.

THIS NEO PART IS LIKE—

INDEED!

総武コミュニティーセンター
SOBU COMMUNITY CENTER.
...I READ YOUR PROPOSAL.
IN ORDER TO FREAK OUT THE PARENTS, WE WANT TO MAKE THE PROM PLAN LOOK AS BIG AS POSSIBLE.
TO THAT END, WINNING OVER KAIHIN GENERAL, AS WELL AS ITS STUDENT COUNCIL PRESIDENT, TAMANAWA, IS THE MOST EFFICIENT APPROACH.
JOINT PROM EVENT
WITH CHIBA KAIHIN AREA
NTARY/MIDDLE/HIGH SCHOO
KAIHIN GENERAL

IT WAS SO PRETENTIOUS, HALFWAY THROUGH, EVEN I HONESTLY DIDN'T KNOW WHAT I WAS WRITING ANYMORE...
I STAYED UP ALL LAST NIGHT WRITING UP A PROPOSAL TO USE ON TAMANAWA...
ATAKAN
JARGON
BLOCKCHAIN-STYLE DIVERSITY INCLUSION PROM NIGHT PROPOSAL
SUNSET BEACH OVERLOOKING THE WATERFRONT, A SERENDIPITOUS EXPERIENCE IN THE ULTIMATE TRANSLUCENT SPACE
FOR A GUY LIKE YOU, IT'S GOT TO HIT HOME...!!
HMM. HMM.
GOKURI (GULP)
ごくり...
HMM.

MAKING ALLOWANCES FOR DIVERSITY IS A GOOD THING, BUT I THINK EVERYTHING ELSE MIGHT BE TOO ABSTRACT. THERE'S TOO MUCH FLUFF, AND THE PLAN IS GENERALLY UNFOCUSED.

WHAT... DID YOU SAY...?

I THINK YOU SHOULD TAKE MORE CARE COMMUNICATING YOUR IDEAS.
I SUPPOSE YOU MIGHT CALL IT THE VISUALIZATION OF A PLAN.
OF COURSE, I CAN UNDERSTAND SETTING YOUR EYE ON FUTURE PROSPECTS FOR THIS KIND OF EXPERIENCE-ORIENTED EVENT...
...BUT YOUR REASONING UP TO THAT POINT DOESN'T STAND.
THAT'S WHY...
SO YOU'RE...
...STILL AT THAT STAGE,
HUH?
...YOUR PROPOSAL IS NO GOOD.

BUT HE LOVED PRETENTIOUS OVERUSE OF ENGLISH TERMS SO MUCH! NOW HE'S TELLING ME NOT TO USE THEM.....?
I CAN'T BELIEVE IT.....
GOOD GRIEF—IT'S SO GOOD, I'D LIKE TO SAY THE SAME THING TO THE OLD TAMANAWA...
AND WHAT'S MORE, HE MADE A TOTALLY SALIENT POINT THAT TARGETED THE HOLES ...
GIRI (GRIT)
BUT, TAMA-NAWA ...
TO (TAP)
TO
GUESS THAT MEANS...
...HE'S GROWN IN HIS OWN WAY, HUH...?

NOW THAT WE'VE BEEN REJECTED BY HAYAMA AND CAN'T WORK WITH THE CAPTAINS' ASSOCIATION, THOUGH...
...I CAN'T BACK DOWN HERE.
I HAVE TO GET TAMANAWA ON BOARD SOMEHOW.
KACHI (CLICK)
KACHI
OUR NEO-PROMJECT...
GATA (SCRAPE)
TAN (TAP)
ZU (SLURP)
NEEDS YOU, OKAY .....!!!?
TAN

IS YOUR PROBLEM WITH OUR PLAN JUST NO BUDGET?
OUR TEAM TAKES PRIDE IN DOING MORE WITH LESS.
WHAT WE GOTTA USE IS A COOL GADGET—
SCALABILITY IS OUR BEST BET!
THIS IS MY BEST SUGGESTION YET!

THE TITLE OF YOUR PLAN IS ABSOLUTELY FRIVOLOUS—
THE CONTENT INSIDE'S SUPERFICIAL AND RIDICULOUS.
SLI (SWF)
IF WE'RE GOING TO PROCEED— YOU, ME, AND ALL OF US...
...WE NEED PRE-CISION, OR IT'LL BE DISAS-TROUS.
BAN! (BAM)
WITHOUT DIRECTION-ALITY, IT'S AWFULLY EGREGIOUS!
FOR WANT OF FURTHER EXPLANATION, THIS WHOLE PROPOSAL'S GONE TO DUST...
...AND THAT'S SOMETHING WE ALL NEED TO DISCUSS.
HUH? THIS IS RANDOM .....

WE DRAFTED WITH GREAT CONSIDERATION —
FOR THE BUDGET, WE LEVERAGE CROWDFUNDING.
WE JUST NEED HANDS AND YOUR REPUTATION.
IT'LL BE EASY WITH THAT INNOVATION!!
I'LL ADMIT THE DIRECTION'S STILL VAGUE ...
...BUT AT THE END OF THE DAY, YOUR KEY TAKEAWAY IS THIS IDEA'S LINCOLN'S PLAY!

WOW...
IT'S TRUE WHAT YOU HAVE INTERESTS ME.
BUT LOOK—YOUR LANGUAGE LEAVES ME DISTRAUGHT.
THE ONLY PART OF YOUR PLAN THAT MATTERS IS THIS PAGE HERE, IN THIS ONE SPOT.
EVERYTHING ELSE YOU'VE WRITTEN READS LIKE A SATIRICAL POTSHOT.
IF WE'RE GOING TO DO THIS TOGETHER, THEN WE'RE ALL IN THE SAME POT.
BUT RIGHT NOW, WE'RE OIL AND WATER, ARE WE NOT?
SO THIS IS FREE-STYLE ...!!

SIGN: SOUBU COMMUNITY CENTER

ZAZAAAN (SPLAAASH)
HACHIMAN... YOU TOOK SO LONG...
GATA (SHIVER)
GATA
SORRY WE'RE LATE.

AGH! COLD, COLD, COLD!
HIKKI, I KINDA HAVE NO IDEA WHAT YOU'RE TALKING ABOUT.
ONCE YOU START RHYMING ON A FOUR-FOUR BEAT, YOU GET INTO A FLOW, AND IT TOOK A LITTLE TIME.
EBINA, GIMME A HOT PAD!!
I SOOOO WANNA GO HOME ALREADY !!
THANK YOU FOR STOPPING HER.
AH... SORRY, FOR REAL...
ON YOUR BACK? OR STOMACH?
BOTH !!
MY SHIVERING WILL NOT RELENT ...

THANKS FOR LENDING US A HAND TODAY. YOU WERE A BIG HELP.
GLAD TO DO SO!
HUH?
SO SCARY.
OKAY, LET'S GET STARTED.
ZAZAAN (WAWOOSH)
KASHA (SNAP)
...
HMM...
Nikou

LET ME TRY?
YOU DO THIS PART LIKE THIS...
...AND THEN GO LIKE THIS!
KI (CLICK)
KA (TIK)
KASHA (SNAP)
OHH, THIS LOOKS KINDA PRO...
RIGHT?
REFLECTION BOARD
YUUMIKOOO!♪
GYEEK!
ZA (SKSH)
AAAND NEXT...

I—
I'LL TAKE MINE OFF MYSELF, OKAY!?
HEY, HEY, HEY! EBINA, YOU JERK!!
HURR HURR HURR! LET IT HAPPEN, LET IT HAPPEEEN! ♪
IF YOU'RE IN UNIFORM ON THE BEACH, YOU'VE REALLY GOT TO BE BAREFOOT! ☆
I GET THAT.
OKAAAY, SAY CHEESE!

THEY'RE ALL PRETTY AND DRESSED UP—THEY'RE A GREAT PAIRING.
OH MY GAAAWD, THE SAND IS SO COOOLD!
I'M NOT GONNA BE IN ANYONE'S OT3.

UH, I MEANT TO GET SHOTS OF YOU TOO WHEN I INVITED YOU, THOUGH.
EHH?

.....WELL, I THINK YOU AND HAYATO COULD BE AN OPTION AS SUBJECTS, THOUGH.
FUJO-HO-HO...
ISN'T THAT SEXUAL HARASS-MENT?

IT'S OKAY, SINCE I'M NOT VERY SEXY.
I DON'T EVEN UNDERSTAND WHAT SEXUAL HARASSMENT FROM SOMEONE WITH NO SEX APPEAL WOULD BE.
UH, YOU'RE MAKING IT KINDA HARD TO ANSWER...
ISN'T THAT HARASSMENT TOO?

WHAT I MEAN IS...
... THINGS LIKE SEX.
OR LOVE, OR ROMANCE...
THEY'RE ALL A HASSLE.

BECAUSE IN THE END...
...BUT, WELL, WON'T THINGS WORK OUT SOME-HOW?
...YOU'RE DIFFERENT FROM ME, HIKIGAYA-KUN.
...DID YOU HEAR SOME-THING?
...
I THINK I'M SORT OF INVOLVED IN IT TOO.
...IT'S OBVIOUS JUST LOOKING AT YOU.

I DON'T KNOW WHY THINGS HAVE GOTTEN LIKE THIS, AND IT'S NOT SOMETHING FOR ME TO SAY.
BUT, LIKE, ISN'T THERE AN EASIER WAY?
...
SIMPLE THINGS ARE THE HARDEST.
IT'S JUST THAT THIS WAS EASIEST FOR ME.
HMM.

...AH, YEAH.
CREEPY.

I'VE BEEN SUM-MONED.
OH, TOO BAD.

LET'S TAKE SOME TOGETHER!
HINAAA!

I DON'T MIND IT AT ALL, YOU KNOW?
THAT SORT OF... PESSIMISM OF YOURS?

WELL ...
...IT'S NOT LIKE I DON'T GET WHAT YOU'RE SAYING, HIKIGAYA-KUN.

...HUH.
PESSIMISM...
AND I CAN SAY THE SAME ABOUT ME AND HER.
THOUGH I CAN SYMPATHIZE, WE REACH DIFFERENT CONCLUSIONS.
NIKON
EBINA AND I REALLY ARE DIFFERENT.
...WON'T THINGS WORK OUT SOMEHOW?
...BUT, WELL...
KASHAN (SNAP)
カシャン

OHH……
ミメ ミメ……
JIJI (TKTK)
WHOA……!!

TOP INFORMATION ABOUT ACCESS CONTACT
JPN
NEO-PROM-JECT
THE TEST UPLOAD IS COMPLETE...!
PHEEEW...!
THANKS FOR YOUR WORK!
COUNTING ON YOU TO UPDATE THE SOCIAL MEDIA, ZAIMO-KUZA.
OKAY, TRANSFERRING TO THE MAIN ENVIRONMENT.
DOES SHE UNDER-STAND THE GOAL HERE ...?
UH, THIS ISN'T ACTUALLY GOING TO HAPPEN, THOUGH...
WAAA!
THIS IS GREAT! I'M KINDA STARTING TO LOOK FORWARD TO THIS!

HIKKI, WHERE ARE YOU GOING?
THIS IS STILL TOO WEAK, IN TERMS OF INFO TRANSMISSION.
I'M GONNA GO LAY SOME INSURANCE, JUST IN CASE.
...MMN. I WAS ALSO CONCERNED ABOUT THAT.
TWEETER PROFESSOR
NO MATTER HOW WE MIGHT TIGHTEN OUR PLANS, WITHOUT RETWEETS OF OUR INFORMATION SOURCE, WE CANNOT EXPECT IT TO SPREAD.
IF THE CONTENT'S GOOD, THAT'S ONE THING, BUT THIS IS A PAPIER-MÂCHÉ PLAN...
IF WE STIR UP TOO MUCH TROUBLE ONLINE, CLEANING THINGS UP AFTER WILL BE A PAIN.
GEE, THIS ALL SOUNDS LIKE SOME DIFFICULT STUFF

...DO YOU HAVE SOME KIND OF MOLE FOR THAT LEAK?
...THE PLAN IS TO HAVE SOMEONE PINPOINT-LEAK TO THE PARENTS.
YEAH, THAT'S WHY...
PLAN ON
SOCIAL MEDIA ACCOU
ZAIMOKUZA
EBSITE
+SAGAMI
TOR
HAMA
ING YOUR NAM
SUGGESTIONS
TE WITH CAPTAIN
N HAYAMA

...BASI-CALLY.
BUT ...

THAT LEAKER IS...
...A BIT TROUBLE-SOME...

TRANSLATION NOTES

Page 10
WAX Coffee is a parody of an actual brand called MAX Coffee.

Page 34
Saizeruya is a reference to the Italian-style family restaurant chain Saizeriya.

Page 37
M-2 Syndrome, or *chuunibyou* in Japanese, refers to the kind of cringey behavior one expects from a second-year middle school student and what someone that age would expect to sound cool and mysterious.

Page 53
Nishi-Chiba Lucky and **Numa Ace** are parody names of arcades in Chiba.

Page 54
"Wait! And hope!" is a line from the novel *The Count of Monte Cristo*, as well as the anime based on it, *Gankutsuou*.

Page 60
-shi is an impersonal honorific used in formal speech or writing, e.g. legal documents. It's another aspect of Zaimokuza's dorky manner of speaking.

Page 109
Destiny Land and **Destiny Sea** are parodies of the Japanese amusement parks Tokyo Disneyland and Tokyo DisneySea.

Page 110
In Japan, the school year typically starts in **April**.

Page 133
Katakana is one of the three writing systems used in the Japanese language and, in modern times, is mostly used for loanwords.

Page 147
"Hurr-hurr-hurr! Let it happen, let it happeeen!" is a stereotypical line in period dramas, often accompanied by the "*obi* spin," where a man yanks on a woman's sash, ripping it off to spin her like a top.

...To Be Continued

① The pattern in Pan-san's eyes is different.
② The pattern of the grass is different.
③ The angle of the grass is different.
④ Yui is wearing a backpack.
⑤ There's one extra button.
⑥ The pizza slicer is facing the other way.
⑦ There's an extra salami slice.
⑧ The shape of the fork is different.
⑨ Sablé's love is one heart stronger.
⑩ "Youth" isn't shiny enough.

YOU'VE HARDLY FOUND ANY OF THEM.
I HAVE ONLY SEVEN MORE TO FIND...

MY YOUTH ROMANTIC COMEDY IS WRONG, AS I EXPECTED @COMIC 18

Original Story: Wataru Watari
Art: Naomichi Io
Character Design: Ponkan⑧
ORIGINAL COVER DESIGN/Hiroyuki KAWASOME (Graphio)

Translation: Jennifer Ward

Lettering: Bianca Pistillo

This book is a work of fiction. Names, characters, places, and incidents are the product of the author's imagination or are used fictitiously. Any resemblance to actual events, locales, or persons, living or dead, is coincidental.

YAHARI ORE NO SEISHUN LOVE COME WA MACHIGATTEIRU. @COMIC Vol. 18 by Wataru WATARI, Naomichi IO, PONKAN⑧
© 2013 Wataru WATARI, Naomichi IO, PONKAN⑧
All rights reserved.
Original Japanese edition published by SHOGAKUKAN.
English translation rights arranged with SHOGAKUKAN through Tuttle-Mori Agency, Inc., Tokyo.

English translation © 2022 by Yen Press, LLC

Yen Press, LLC supports the right to free expression and the value of copyright. The purpose of copyright is to encourage writers and artists to produce the creative works that enrich our culture.

The scanning, uploading, and distribution of this book without permission is a theft of the author's intellectual property. If you would like permission to use material from the book (other than for review purposes), please contact the publisher. Thank you for your support of the author's rights.

Yen Press
150 West 30th Street, 19th Floor
New York, NY 10001

Visit us at yenpress.com
facebook.com/yenpress
twitter.com/yenpress
yenpress.tumblr.com
instagram.com/yenpress

First Yen Press Edition: July 2022
Edited by Yen Press Editorial: Carl Li
Designed by Yen Press Design: Wendy Chan

Yen Press is an imprint of Yen Press, LLC.
The Yen Press name and logo are trademarks of Yen Press, LLC.

The publisher is not responsible for websites (or their content) that are not owned by the publisher.

Library of Congress Control Number: 2016931004

ISBNs: 978-1-9753-4789-5 (paperback)
978-1-9753-4790-1 (ebook)

10 9 8 7 6 5 4 3 2 1

WOR

Printed in the United States of America